omit chapter on European civilisation to page 219.

THE TWO SABBATHS:

AN ESSAY

SHOWING THAT THE PATRIARCHAL AND CHRISTIAN SABBATH ARE ONE AND THE SAME

AND THAT

THE JEWISH SABBATH HAS BEEN ABROGATED.

BY

REV. E. Q. FULLER.

CINCINNATI:
PUBLISHED BY POE & HITCHCOCK.

R. P. THOMPSON, PRINTER.
1864.

PREFACE.

In the following pages there is less of novelty than might perhaps be expected from a reading of the title-page, or of the Propositions discussed. The arguments brought forward are based upon generally-admitted facts, or such as are accredited by men noted for learning and ability. And though these facts are placed in somewhat new relations, it is believed that they are only given their proper bearings. Great care has been taken, in the numerous quotations given, to present the author's true and complete sense, though, in many cases, they may not have been aware that such use can so easily be made of their statements. There having been a constant aim to present the discussion in the smallest suitable compass, quotations have been made brief as the sense would allow, while to aid the inquirer several authors are merely referred to.

It is not claimed that the authors quoted or referred to advocate the Propositions herein brought forward. The writer is not aware that all of them have before been laid down; but these authors have made a foundation upon which he has built, and, confident in the learning and wisdom of others, it is hoped that the structure is firm.

Some dependence is made, it will be seen, upon chronological data as found in the Scriptures. Perhaps this may be counted unreliable. If so, let it be asked, Is the Bible true? Certainly. Then we have an exact chronology from the creation to Christ, which, when interpreted aright, will become plain.

The arguments drawn from heathen mythology, found under the Third Proposition, Second Section, may receive special attention, and deserve to be dwelt upon more fully. At first sight, the harmony made to appear between different branches of pagan philosophy will perhaps be questioned, but upon inspection it will be found correct.

Humbly believing that in what follows is indicated, if not given, a satisfactory solution of the difficult problems of the Divine authority of the Christian Sabbath, these few pages are submitted to public scrutiny, trusting that the hours of research required for their preparation will prove to have been given to the edification of the Church.

E. Q. F.

AURORA, ILLINOIS.

PROPOSITIONS DISCUSSED.

V.

VI.

THE TWO SABBATHS.

INTRODUCTION.

Title explained—Six Propositions named—Real and clock time—The *day* of Sabbath easily determined—The Sabbath a physical and moral necessity.

WHAT is here to be understood by the terms "the *two* Sabbaths," is, first, that the Sabbath, hallowed at the creation of the world, is a perpetual institution, the weekly observance of which was from the beginning, and will be, till the ending of time, binding upon the entire race of man, excepting the Jews during the period of their national history; that it is the *present Christian Sabbath;* and, second, that the Jewish Sabbath was an extraordinary, a temporary institution pertaining alone to the Mosaic economy, originating in and ending with it.

In support of these views it will be maintained in the following pages: *First*, that a perpetual Sabbath was instituted at the creation of the world. *Second*, that the original Sabbath was on the first day of the week. *Third*, that the original Sabbatic law has ever been, and does now remain, in full force to all people but the Jews, who were exempted from its weekly observance from the exodus to the crucifixion. *Fourth*, that at the exodus the seventh day of the week was appointed a peculiar Sabbath for the Jews. *Fifth*, that the Jewish Sabbath was abrogated with the Jewish economy. And, *Sixth*, that when Judaism was abrogated the original Sabbath remained to the Christian Church.

Before entering upon a discussion of these propositions it may be observed that the difference between *real* time and *clock* time, or difference in the longitude of various places where a reckoning of the Sabbath may be made, does not, as has been contended by some, negative this whole question by confusing the days of the week. Time is reckoned from the creation of Adam. This was the last of the sixth day's work; so that with Adam's life the seventh day of creation, named in Gen. ii, 1–3, but the *first* day of *time*, began, probably at sunset, as the Jews calculate, of the sixth day. Ever after sunset would mark the closing of one day and the beginning of another. Fifteen degrees west of Eden, or any given place, the day would begin later by one hour of *real* or absolute time, but at the same moment of *clock* or mean time; namely, at sunset. Thus east or west the day would begin earlier or later by real time according to the longitude of the place given; but every-where at the setting of the sun. And seven days or a hundred thousand years from the creation the requisite number of *sunsets* would mark the beginning of the Sabbath in any part of the world. Of course, it is not claimed that each recurring Sabbath can now be traced through all the past; but in the following discussion admitted facts will be brought forward to show that neither the weekly period nor the first-day Sabbath has ever been lost. Besides, Providence seems to have especially guarded this matter; "Westward the star of empire" moves, and has moved since the banishment of man from Eden. No nation has ever emigrated so far eastward as to cause their weekly reckoning to conflict with that of their neighbors upon the west. The East and West had never met till the Chinese came to California. If the day was originally computed from the meridian sun, or, as with us, from midnight, the foregoing conclusion would remain unshaken.

It should also be remembered that to man in his present state, if, indeed, not in Paradise, the Sabbath is a physical and moral necessity. We are commanded to do no work on that day because man and beast require it as a day of rest. "It is essentially necessary," says Dr. Clarke, "not only to the body of man, but to all the animals employed in his service; take this away and the labor is too great; both man and beast would fail under it." This thought is well considered in the "Sabbath Manual."

The Sabbath is equally necessary to man for moral purposes. The public worship of God is enjoined on that day, because society can not be preserved in the knowledge and love of God without stated public worship of God. Rev. J. C. Ryle very aptly remarks, "Once give over caring for the Sabbath, and in the end you will give over caring for your soul. The steps which lead to this conclusion are easy and regular. Begin with not honoring God's day, and you will soon not honor God's house. Cease to honor God's house, and you will soon cease to honor God's book. Cease to honor God's book, and by and by you will give God no honor at all. Let a man lay the foundation of having no Sabbath, and I am never surprised if he finish with the top-stone of NO GOD. It is a remarkable saying of Judge Hale," continues Mr. Ryle, "of all the persons who were convicted of capital crimes while he was upon the bench, he found only a few who would not confess, on inquiry, that they began the career of their wickedness by a neglect of the Sabbath." "Without this consecrated day," again quoting from Dr. Clarke, "religion itself would fail, and the human mind becoming secularized would soon forget its origin and end. Even as a *political* regulation, it is one of the wisest and most beneficent in its effects of any ever instituted. Those who habitually disregard its moral obligation are, to a man, not only good for nothing, but are wretched in themselves, a curse to society, and often end their lives miserably." (Com., vol. i, p. 39.) Of all these facts the history of the world affords conclusive evidence. How strong, then, the presumption that the world would not be left in any period of its history without such an institution! And from this consideration alone no little measure of plausibility is given to the mass of argument found in this essay.

FIRST PROPOSITION.

A PERPETUAL SABBATH WAS INSTITUTED AT THE CREATION OF THE WORLD.

Scripture testimony—Cain and Abel—Noah—Job—Jacob—The Israelites—"Statutes of Adam"—Dr. Kennicott's views—Testimony of the ancients.

THE discussion of a proposition so generally admitted might be deemed unnecessary; but it is often denied, and should, therefore, be considered with no little care.

Immediately after the account of the creation of the world the Sacred Record says: "On the seventh day God ended his work which he had made; and he rested on the seventh day from all his work which he had made; and God blessed the seventh day, and sanctified it: because that in it he had rested from all his work." Gen. ii, 2, 3. It has been contended that the Sabbath is here named merely in anticipation of such a "*rest*" as an institution to be ordained at some future time. But it is here claimed that the Sabbath is explicitly named in this language as instituted on the seventh day of creation, the first day of time; and it is reasonable to infer that it was designed by the Creator to be religiously observed by all mankind forever.

This position is fully warranted by the language of the Decalogue. The fourth commandment reads: "Remember the Sabbath day to keep it holy; for in six days the Lord made heaven and earth, and all that in them is, and rested the seventh day: wherefore the Lord blessed the Sabbath day; and hallowed it." "Remember" an old institution, and "remember" it always. Remember it also *because* the Lord "rested" on, and "blessed," that particular day of the week, and, further, remember it often as it recurs. So, in Nehemiah ix, 14, it is written: Thou "*madest known* unto them thy holy Sabbath," "as if," says Dr. Clarke, the

Jews "had forgotten it in Egypt." This passage from the law clearly shows that the day first succeeding the work of creation was "hallowed," agreeable to the evident meaning of the third verse of the second chapter of Genesis; also, that the Sabbath was a permanent institution, to be remembered forever.

Further evidence that there was instituted at the creation a perpetual weekly Sabbath is found in the history of Cain and Abel, Noah, Job, Jacob, and the departure of the Israelites from Egypt.

Cain and Abel offered sacrifices "in process of time," or "at the end of days," (marg.;) that is, at the *end* of the six working days, as the new week began. Gen. iv, 3. On this passage Dr. Clarke remarks, "It is probable that it means the *Sabbath* on which Adam and his family undoubtedly offered oblations to God, as the Divine worship was certainly instituted, and no doubt the Sabbath properly observed in that family." (Com., vol. i, p. 56.)

Noah sent out the raven and the dove from the ark every seventh day, and upon the Sabbath, as will hereafter appear. Gen. viii, 6–12. Of these incidents Matthew Henry says: "Noah sent forth the dove after seven days, and, probably, the first sending of her out was seven days after the sending forth of the raven, which intimated that it was done on the Sabbath day, which, it would seem, Noah religiously observed in the ark." Comp. Com., vol. i, p. 58.

It is probable that Job also had a correct knowledge of the weekly Sabbath. He "offered burnt-offerings . . . . continually," or "all the days," (marg.;) that is, either all the sacred days, or daily. Job i, 5. "Job, like Abraham," says Henry, "had a family altar, on which, it is likely, he offered sacrifices daily." Comp. Com., vol. ii, pp. 597, 598. Considering that this patriarch was eminently pious, and that the Sabbath was known before him till after the Flood, and after him before the giving of the law on Sinai, as will soon appear; and considering that he and his friends did observe the weekly period—Job ii, 13—is it not reasonable to conclude that he knew and religiously kept the holy Sabbath?

In the days of Jacob the "week" was well known, and is spoken of in the Scripture as being generally familiar at the time of his marriage. Gen. xxix, 27, 28. Dr. Scott observes, "The division of time by weeks intimates that some regard was paid to the Sabbath;" namely, in these ages—the times of Noah and Jacob. Comp. Com., vol. i, p. 136; Scott's Com. on Gen. ii, 2, 3; viii, 6–14; xxix, 27, 28; Ex. xx, 8–11. Indeed, it would have been impossible for the weekly period to have been thus preserved, as inspiration demonstrates it to have been, through all those remote ages, without the preservation of the memory of the sacred day by a suitable observation of its rites. See Gurney on the Sabbath, chap. i.

After the Israelites left Egypt at the exodus, and sixteen days before the giving of the law from Sinai, we have, in the sixteenth chapter of the book of Exodus, the following account of the observance of the Sabbath on the *seventh* day of the week, instead of the *first* day: "Then said the Lord unto Moses, Behold, I will rain bread from heaven for you; and the people shall go out and gather a certain rate every day, that I may prove them, whether they will walk in my law, or no. And it shall come to pass, that on the sixth day they shall prepare that which they bring in; and it shall be twice as much as they gather daily." Ex. xvi, 4, 5.

"And it came to pass, that on the sixth day they gathered twice as much bread, two omers for one man: and all the rulers of the congregation came and told Moses. And he said unto them, This is that which the Lord hath said, To-morrow [the *seventh*, and not the *first*, day] is the rest of the holy Sabbath unto the Lord: bake that which ye will bake to-day, and seethe that ye will seethe; and that which remaineth over, lay up for you to be kept until the morning. And they laid it up till the morning, as

Moses bade: and it did not stink, neither was there any worm therein. And Moses said, Eat that to-day; for to-day is a Sabbath unto the Lord: to-day ye shall not find it in the field. Six days ye shall gather it; but on the seventh day, which is the Sabbath, in it there shall be none. And it came to pass, that there went out some of the people on the seventh day to gather, and they found none. And the Lord said unto Moses, How long refuse ye to keep my commandments and my laws? See, for that the Lord hath given you the Sabbath, therefore he giveth you on the sixth day the bread of two days: abide ye every man in his place, let no man go out of his place on the seventh day. So the people rested on the *seventh* day." Ex. xvi, 22–30.

Here is a plain account of Sabbath observance before the reception of the Decalogue. That, however, the Sabbath was not here first instituted is evident, not only from the foregoing arguments, but also from the text itself. The manna was so given as to prove Israel, particularly in respect to the law of the Sabbath, which we are left to infer had been before appointed. Speaking upon this passage, Dr. Clarke says, there is nothing in the text "that seems to intimate that the Sabbath was now first given to the Israelites; on the contrary, it is here spoken of as being perfectly well known," (Com., vol. i, p. 384,) except in the day upon which it was hereafter to fall. Dr. Scott adds, "The whole narrative implies that reference was made to an institution before known but not properly remembered or regarded, and not to any *new law* given on the occasion. Neither the inquiry of the elders nor the language of Moses can be consistently interpreted of an entirely new institution." Matthew Henry says, "We have a plain intimation of the observing of a seventh day [that is, a weekly] Sabbath, not only before the giving of the law on Mount Sinai, but before the bringing of Israel out of Egypt, and, therefore, from the beginning." Comp. Com., vol. i,

p. 274, and Note. Also Scott's Com., vol. i, pp. 235–238. That there was, however, something *new* to the Israelites, in this revival of the Sabbath, is evident from the text. That novelty, *to wit*, the change from the first to the seventh day, will be hereafter more fully considered.

Many celebrated ancient authors and learned antiquarians have held, with good reasons, that the substance of the whole Decalogue was contained in a moral code known as the "Statutes of Adam," or the "Precepts of the sons of Noah;" and that this code was extant ages before the time of Moses. It is certain that the world has never been without both a form of religion and a Divine revelation. The seventh article of this code, as given in the "Sacred Annals," is in these words; namely, "To observe the Sabbath as a day of sacred rest and worship."

In proof of this point, Dr. Kennicott, as quoted by the same author, has laid down the following propositions which he has argued with great force:

"1. That this blessing and sanctifying of the seventh day [in the seventh day of creation named in Gen. ii, 2, 3] contained an order from God to Adam and his posterity to observe a weekly Sabbath, or one day in seven, after a holy manner.

"2. That, though this command was reënforced by a more awful delivery of it from Mount Sinai, yet it was expressly observed by the children of Israel before that delivery of it from Mount Sinai.

"3. That this observation of theirs must have been in obedience to some positive institution; and, as there is no intermediate or second institution, it could only be in obedience to this first institution, which consequently continued in force down to the delivery of the law from Sinai.

"4. That the same institution was observed during the ante-Mosaic economy, and that this Sabbath was the day on which Cain and Abel came together to offer their oblations to the Deity." (Kennicott's Obl., Cain and Abel.)

The following quotations prove that, unless all nations, "throughout the whole world," borrowed the Sabbatic institution from the Jews, it *must* have been handed down from the patriarchs—through Noah from Adam. That it was borrowed from the Jews is a supposition without a shadow of proof, and unreasonable; besides, these quotations show that it could not have been thus borrowed because it is evidently older than Judaism.

Josephus says, "There is no city, Greek or barbarian, in which the custom of resting on the seventh day is not preserved."

On these words of Josephus, Selden remarks, that "it proves the *universal* computation of time by weeks."

Philo, speaking of the Sabbath, observes: "It is a festival celebrated not only in one city or country, but throughout the *whole world.*"

"Aristobulus," says Calmet, "quotes Homer and Hesiodes, who speak of the seventh day as sacred and venerable. Clemens Alexandrinus adds some passages from the ancients who celebrate the seventh day. Some rabbins inform us that Joseph also observed the Sabbath in Egypt." (Calmet's Dict.)

Watson corroborates Calmet. He says, "Plain intimations of this weekly revolution of time are to be found in the earliest Greek poets, Hesiod, Homer, Linus, as well as among the nations of the Chaldeans, Egyptians, Greeks, and Romans." (Theo. Dict.)

The testimony of Grotius is very direct. He says: "The memory of the six days' work [of creation] was preserved, not only among the Greeks and Italians, by honoring the seventh day, but also among the Celtæ and Indians, who all measure the time by weeks."

"When we remember," observes an able writer, "that all the patriarchs, from Adam to Moses, had set times for their solemn assemblies, and these times were weekly and of Divine institution; that, upon the return of these weekly Sabbaths, very probably it was that Cain and

Abel offered their respective sacrifices to God; and that Noah, the only righteous person among [the last generation of] the antediluvians, Abraham, the most faithful servant of God after the Flood, and Job, that 'perfect and upright' man, are all supposed to have observed it; we can not but think that the day whereon the work of creation was concluded, from the very beginning of time, was every week—till men had corrupted their ways—kept holy as being the birthday of the world, and the universal festival of mankind." (Stackhouse's Hist. Bib. See Sac. Annals, vol. i, pp. 217–222.)

Is it not reasonably established that the holy Sabbath, as a permanent institution, was ordained at the creation of the world? Other facts, however, omitted for the present to avoid repetition, will be given, which might have been used here with much force. Special attention is called to numerous quotations in the small, but able, work of Gurney already referred to.

SECOND PROPOSITION.

THE ORIGINAL SABBATH WAS ON THE FIRST DAY OF THE WEEK.

Time began when creation was completed—Life of Adam—The seventh day of the creation week was the first day of time—That day observed by the patriarchs—Strangely marked in the Jewish economy—The Sun's day of the heathen was the Sabbath of the patriarchs.

THE existence of the Sabbath presupposes, as Selden remarks, the computation of time by weeks. As Grotius says, the memory of the six days' work of creation was preserved in the weekly period. The week, then, is as old as the reckoning of time, which was from the earliest hour there was one to compute it from any definite and apparent starting-point, as sunset of the sixth day. For already there were in the heavens "lights" "for signs and for seasons, for days and years." Gen. i, 14. The first day counted would naturally be the first day of the week. That day was the Sabbath, called in the history of the creation the "seventh day," which God "blessed" and "sanctified."

Chronology does not commence with the "beginning" of creation, but with the completion of it. Time is reckoned in the Scriptures from the creation of Adam; thus, Adam "*lived* a hundred and thirty years, and begat Seth." This is agreeable to Josephus, who computed time from the same event. How can there be any prior computation? Before him was eternity, not time—duration not having been measured or "cut off" by human history. Adam was created last of all the Divine handiwork, at the very close, we may suppose, of the sixth day. The next, the seventh from the beginning of creation, must have been the first of his existence, and, as chronology begins with his existence, this "seventh" day of God's work, which he "blessed" and "sanctified," upon which Adam first appeared before his Maker "very good," *must have* been the first day of the week and of the year, because, being the first day in the history of man, it was strictly the first day of time. Time could not have been reckoned till man was placed upon the earth, certainly not historic time. To compute chronology from a period prior to Adam would be absurd—a beginning of history not only before there were events to record, but before even an ancestry of the actors were in being. It is not considered here whether the days of creation, mentioned by Moses, were equal in duration to twenty-four hours or not. Be that as it may, it can not alter the fact stated, because these days are not, nor can they be, included in the history of our race. This Proposition, then, from the nature of the case, is found to be true. The fact is set forth because it could not have been otherwise. (See Bib. Chro., p. 111.)

Further, Cain and Abel observed this *day of the week*, offering their sacrifices "at the end of days,"* that is, after the ending of the six working days, as the week had closed and a new one began—on the first day of the week. Noah did the same, sending forth the raven and the dove, not only on every seventh day, but upon the original Sabbath. According to the chronology of the Septuagint—confessedly the most reliable, and probably correct—(see Sac. An. Ant. Chro.) it is found that Noah sent out these birds on the first day of the original week—the Sabbath—the tenth, seventeenth, and twenty-fourth of the eleventh month, and the first of the twelfth month of the original year, synchronizing with *Sundays*, the twentieth and twenty-seventh of July, and the third and the tenth of August, 1430, A. J. P. (Bib. Chro., p. 120.) On the Sabbath, "in the six hundred and first year"—of Noah's life—"in the first month and the first day of the month, the waters were dried up from off the earth; and Noah removed the covering

* For an illustration of this time see page 57.

of the ark, and looked, and behold, the face of the ground was dry." Gen. viii, 13. This patriarch did not then look upon a new earth in all its perfection, "very good," as did Adam when he appeared before the Lord on the first Sabbath, but he saw the world cleansed from its wickedness, and a type of the "new earth wherein dwelleth righteousness." And he, looking from the ark upon the earth purified by water, was a type of Him who came, upon the same day, from the grave, upon the earth redeemed by blood. It is also claimed, by some, that Noah both entered the ark and removed from it on the first day of the original week—the Sabbath. If so, he "rested" from the dangers of the flood upon the same day that God "rested" from the work of creation, the Jews "rested" from bondage, and Christ "rested" from the work of redemption.

The sixth and seventh days of the week, mentioned in the sixteenth chapter of Exodus, when the manna was first given, synchronize with the same days of the original week, thus showing that this period had been carefully preserved from the beginning. (Bib. Chro., pp. 98–121.) So that, as was just said, on this day the children of Israel first rested from bondage. The wave-sheaf, also, was offered, the law given on Sinai, the Pentecost occurred yearly, the Savior arose from the dead, the Spirit was poured upon the Church upon this first day of the week.

The Sun's-day of the heathen, always synchronizing with the first day of the week—the Christian Sabbath — is the holy Sabbath perverted; and is found, as has been seen, to synchronize with the patriarchal institution as early as the Flood. Selden says, "Sunday was the first day of the week in the East from all antiquity." (Sac. An., vol. i, p. 221.) The peculiar regard bestowed upon that day by the heathen further proves it to have ever been the first day of the week, and of patriarchal origin, also a perversion of the original holy Sabbath. This will more fully appear in the discussion of the next Proposition.

Can any thing be more evident, unless it be matter of direct Divine revelation, or of mathematical certainty, than the truthfulness of this Proposition?

THIRD PROPOSITION.

SECTION FIRST.

THE ORIGINAL SABBATIC LAW HAS EVER BEEN, AND DOES NOW REMAIN, IN FULL FORCE TO ALL PEOPLE BUT THE JEWS; WHO WERE EXEMPTED FROM ITS WEEKLY OBSERVANCE FROM THE EXODUS TO THE CRUCIFIXION.

This law has not been repealed—Judaism and the first-day Sabbath—The Decalogue given—The Israelites "rest"—The wave-sheaf—The Pentecost—The Passover and appointment of the seventh-day Sabbath.

IT is already proven that the Sabbath "blessed" at the creation of the world was a permanent institution, as Dr. Kennicott says, for "Adam and all his posterity." Our Lord teaches the same truth when he says, "The Sabbath was made for man." Mark ii, 27. Watson so understands this text, saying upon it, "Not for the Jews only, or for any other class of men, but for MAN; for man even in his innocence and purity, and, therefore, for all his descendants." (Mat. Exp., p. 329. See also Kitto's Cyclo., Art. Sabbath.)

Now, should any deny this Third Proposition, it would devolve upon him to show, in contradiction to the text above quoted, when and where this law has been repealed. But this can not be shown, for the simple reason that it has in no way been annulled. It does, therefore, yet stand in full force.

So far was the Jewish economy from annulling the original law of the Sabbath, that it carefully preserved the patriarchal institution distinct from the Jewish, as the following facts so clearly show. The Decalogue, though pronounced *to* the Jews, was not *for* them alone; but its commands are binding upon the race. That enjoins upon the *race* the duty of remembering the Sabbath, "*for* in six days the Lord made heaven and earth." The original Sabbath is here directly referred to and required to be kept in perpetual remembrance by Jew and Gentile. Apparently for the purpose of distinguishing this day in the most solemn manner, never to be forgotten, after the preparation of Friday and Saturday, God appeared in majesty upon the Mount on the first day of the week, the patriarchal Sabbath, and gave the law, through the Jews, to the whole world. "His"—Moses—"*first* return" from Sinai "was on the Jewish Sabbath; when all was broken, and proved unprofitable. But his *second* return was on the Jewish first day of the week; or, as we have it in the New Testament, on the 'Lord's day.'" (Bib. Chro., pp. 213–218.)

The children of Israel left Egypt on Saturday—Bib. Chro., p. 211—so they first "rested" from bondage on the original Sabbath; thus again marking that day in a singular and typical manner, prefiguring thereby the "rest" of the Church from the bondage of the temple service—from the letter that killeth.

The *wave-sheaf* was a type of the resurrection of Christ; the "*first-fruits* of them that slept," and was offered on the morrow after the Jewish Sabbath. Lev. xxiii, 10, 11. See also Clarke's Com., vol. vi, pp. 282, 283; Barnes on 1 Cor., pp. 312, 313; Horne's Int., vol. ii, pp. 119, 120; West's An. Bib., p. 173, Notes. This offering, then, was made upon the first day of the week, and signified that Christ should be raised from the dead, and "rest;" the work of the redemption being finished, and the new world or new creation begun on that day. This offering of the wave-sheaf kept in constant memory a perpetual Sabbath of *rest*—not burdened with bloody rites as was the Jewish—as has been all along intimated, the particular day on which God "rested" from the work of creation, on which Noah "rested" from the Flood, on which Israel "rested" from bondage, and on which Christ should "rest" from his work, and on which the Church should "rest" in all ages after him, enjoying the literal "rest" which the apostle Paul said yet remained, and type of that everlasting "rest," or Sabbath, now remaining.

The Pentecost, also, occurred on the morrow after the Jewish Sabbath, on the first day of the week. Lev. xxiii, 15, 16. This feast was instituted in memory of the descent of God upon Sinai to deliver the law on the fiftieth day after the exodus or eating of the paschal lamb. Christ being the real paschal sacrifice, the Pentecost foreshadowed some glorious manifestation of the Divine presence to, or upon, the Church the fiftieth day after Christ was offered. Here, then, in connection with this feast we have the perpetual Sabbath still further marked by the awful revelations of Sinai, the yearly observance of the Pentecost, and, finally, unmistakably linked to the new dispensation by the gift of the Holy Ghost in "tongues as of fire" upon the apostles upon the first day of the week. See Clarke's Com., vol. i, p. 395; vol. vi, p. 690; Wat.'s Dict., Art. Pentecost. West's An. Bib., p. 173, Notes.

The day "sanctified" at the beginning of time

has now been traced through all the patriarchal ages and the Mosaic economy to the establishment of the Christian Church; and here, for the present, is left the Scripture history of the institution.

The Jews, let it be remembered, were not permitted to lose sight wholly of this day. Its occasional observance has already been pointed out; but it is clear that they were ordinarily required to keep but one day in each week in a sacred manner. That day is universally acknowledged to have been, through all their national history, the seventh day of the week. Their exemption, then, from the weekly observance of the first day is, beyond controversy, of Divine appointment. This exemption is at least implied in the consecration of the seventh day at the exodus, which is admirably set forth in the following words of Dr. Akers: "The months of a Scriptural year have never exceeded twelve. These were originally composed of thirty days each, except the twelfth, which had thirty-five, and every fourth year they gave it thirty-six days. The Alexandrine copy of the Septuagint, the only defensible copy of the Scriptures, as to their chronology down to the exodus, with a single obvious correction of sixty years in the age of Terah, at the birth of Abraham, makes the exode of Israel out of Egyptian bondage occur on the fifteenth day of the seventh month, A. M. 3899. And if this number be divided by a solar cycle of twenty-eight years, formed on the basis of twelve months, as above stated, it will prove that the original seventh-day Sabbath of the Lord [the first day of the week] recurred for that month on the sixteenth day — the day next following the exode of Israel.

"A new calendar was then given to the Israelites. The fifteenth day of this month, Abib, was distinguished from all other days for its importance in the history of the Jews. 'And this day shall be unto you for a memorial; and ye shall keep it a feast unto the Lord throughout your generations: ye shall keep it a feast by an ordinance forever, for in this self-same day have I brought your armies out of the land of Egypt: therefore ye shall observe this day in your generations by an ordinance forever.' Ex. xii, 14–18. 'In the fourteenth day of the first month at even is the Lord's Passover, and on the fifteenth day of the same month is the feast of unleavened bread unto the Lord.' Lev. xxiii, 5, 6; Numb. xxviii, 17. These quotations prove, first, that, though the Passover lambs were to be slain on the fourteenth, they were not to be eaten till 'the night' or evening came, which made both the Passover and first day of unleavened bread, and also the departure of Israel out of bondage, occur on the said fifteenth day of Abib. And, second, it is thus proved that on the same day was the first commemorative and typical feast appointed to be observed by the Jews annually, throughout their generations. This may serve to show the distinguished importance which was attached to this day, in their future history, as suggested in their obligation to 'remember it.'

And now I shall attempt to prove that it was no less distinguished for being the stationary, weekly Sabbath, from which, and to which, all others were to be counted and conformed through the months of the whole year." (Bib. Chro., pp. 98–100.)

Conclusively this author proves this day to have been such a Sabbath throughout all the generations of Israel, and its appointment as such, under the circumstances, implies an exemption from the weekly observance of the first day, as has been said. All other nations, and even the Jews after the fulfillment and abrogation of the ceremonial Sabbath, are held to a constant and perpetual observance of the primitive one, which has now become the Christian Sabbath.

THIRD PROPOSITION.

SECTION SECOND.

PERPETUAL OBLIGATION OF THE SABBATIC LAW.

The week, its origin—Origin of the names of the days of the week—Temple of the "Seven Spheres"—Sunday—Monday—Tuesday—Wednesday—Thursday—Friday—Saturday—The sacred numbers, three, four, seven, and twelve.

THE third Proposition is so evidently founded in truth that it need not, perhaps, be further considered. But there is yet a greatly-neglected field of inquiry relating directly to all the Propositions discussed, which shall be reviewed as fully as these limits will allow. That field of inquiry is the religions of the heathen.

No system of religion was ever invented, really, by man. All false religions, in their essential features, are founded in perversions of

Divine truth, or, as saith the apostle, a "changing of the truth of God into a lie." The names of the days of the week, now in use among us, afford a striking illustration of this fact. An examination of them, severally, will show that the Sabbath, as already claimed, was instituted in the earliest period of the world's history, was the first day of the week, and was a permanent religious institution handed down—perverted, it is true—but handed down through heathenism to this age; that the patriarchal and Christian Sabbath and heathen Sunday were, at the first, one and the same. This testimony harmonizes perfectly with the teaching of Scripture. So forcible is the evidence to be thus gathered, and so independent of that already given, that, if that were wanting, this would afford a sufficient basis on which to rest both the faith and practice of the Church in regarding the first day of the week as peculiarly sacred.

In beginning another train of argument, a few thoughts respecting the weekly period may well be added here. "The week," says another author, "had its origin with the commencement of time; when after six days employed in the work of creation, God rested on the seventh, and blessed it, and set it apart to be continually as a day of holy rest, and a sacred memorial of that great event. . . . It has happened that some traces of the ancient week are to be found in every quarter of the world. Nations the most distant from each other, and of every character, have united in giving testimony to the truth of the Bible account; either by retaining, in their common reckoning of time, the regular division of seven days, or, at least, by showing such regard to that definite period as can in no way be accounted for, if it was not received by tradition from the earliest ages. Not only has this been the case in all the countries of the East, such as Egypt, Arabia, Assyria, India, China, and others; but among the most ancient people of Europe also, the Greeks, the Romans, the Gauls, the Germans, the Britons, and several nations of the North—and this long before they had any knowledge of Christianity, as is evident from the *names* of the days found in use among them, which were of idolatrous origin. Even among the uncultivated tribes of Africa, travelers have met with the same division of time. It is not only, however, by retaining the number of days which compose a week that the tradition of the world so evidently confirms the account of Moses; the testimony is rendered still more striking by the very general idea of some *peculiar sacredness belonging to the seventh day*, which has existed in every age." (Nevin's Bib. Antiq.)

By the term "seventh day" the writer here evidently means simply one day in seven. Different nations have to some extent differed, it is true, as to which one of the days was *most* sacred, as they have as to which one of their gods was most adorable. But the day standing preeminently above all others as *the* sacred one, the world over, is Sunday. "What is remarkable," says the Ency. Amer., "the days of the week are generally named after the sun and planets, only six planets having been known to the ancients." These names are not only generally the same, but, so far as the writer has been able to ascertain, always so, in all times and languages—excepting the Jewish numerals—and in the following order; namely, Sun, Moon, Mars, Mercury, Jupiter, Venus, and Saturn. "In ancient Egyptian astronomy, the order of the planets, in respect of distance from the earth, beginning with the most remote, is, Saturn, Jupiter, Mars, the Sun, Venus, Mercury, the Moon. The day was divided into twenty-four hours, and each successive hour consecrated to a particular planet in the order now stated; so that one hour being consecrated to Saturn, the next would fall to Jupiter, the third to Mars, and so on; and each day was named after the planet to which its first hour was consecrated. Now, suppose the first hour of a particular day to have been consecrated to Saturn, it is evident that

Saturn would also have the eighth, fifteenth, and twenty-second hours. The twenty-third hour would, therefore, fall to Jupiter; the twenty-fourth to Mars; and the twenty-fifth, or the first hour of the following day, would belong to the Sun, from which it [the day] would take its name. By proceeding in the same manner it is found that the first hour of the third day would fall to the Moon, the fourth to Mars, the fifth to Mercury, the sixth to Jupiter, and the seventh to Venus. The cycle being completed, the first hour of the eighth day would return to Saturn, and all the others constantly succeed in the same order." (Brande's Ency., Art. Week.) Beginning with Saturday, we have here the order of the days of the week as they now stand in our calendar, and as they have stood in our calendar, and as they have stood in the calendars of Christendom and of heathen nations through all historic time. Here is doubtless the explanation of the statements of Dio Casius and Diodorus Siculus, that *Saturday* was the first day of the week with the Egyptians. But if we were to commence with Sunday, or any other day, the order would be the same. We have simply brought to view two points of reckoning, one from the most distant planet known, Saturn; the other, which seems far the most natural, both from the most luminous of the heavenly bodies, the Sun, and the most memorable event known, the true beginning period, the creation. It may be that the exodus of Israel may have had something to do with this apparent disorder.

In the "Temple of the Seven Spheres," in Babylon, we have the same order of the planets, from which we deduce by the same process a like order of the days of the week. Sir Henry Rawlinson, by excavations made in 1854, ascertained that this structure—supposed by many to be the same as the Temple of Belus, but probably one of Ashteroth—consisted of six distinct platforms or terraces. Each terrace was about twenty feet in hight, and forty-two feet less horizontally than the one below it. Upon the sixth story stands what is supposed to be the sanctum of the temple. Each stage was dedicated to a planet, and stained with the color peculiarly attributed to it by the Sabian astrologers. The lowest stage was colored black, in honor of Saturn; the second orange, for Jupiter; the third red, for Mars; the fourth yellow, for the Sun; the fifth green, for Venus; the sixth blue, for Mercury; and the temple was probably white, for the Moon, agreeable to the Egyptian astronomy as above.

These names had not exclusively an astronomical origin or import; but were from the first embodiments of religious belief. The remarkable agreement in the religious ideas found in them, in so many varied systems, languages, and periods of time, amounts to a demonstration that they had a common origin before the confusion of tongues and the dispersion from Babel. The primary meaning of the sacred numbers, three, four, seven, and twelve, seems also to find an illustration in them, a further evidence of their great antiquity. Let each name now be separately considered.

Sunday is "so called because anciently dedicated to the Sun." (Webster.) This name is found with little variation in Saxon, German. Dutch, Danish, Gothic, Sanscrit, Sclavonic, Irish, and Welsh; in Latin, *Dies Solis* and *Dies Dominica*—Sun's-day and Lord's-day. The fourth stage of the "Temple of the Seven Spheres" is colored yellow or golden for the sun, symbolizing light, splendor, excellence, purity, and vitality. This day is named from the sun in most of the languages of the earth according to authorities already quoted.

God, the Father, the first person of the Holy Trinity, revealed himself to Adam, as CREATOR. Very soon after the Flood, if not indeed before, man basely worshiped the *creature* more than the *Creator*. The sun being the fountain of light, and the apparent cause of life in the earth, was the creature that came to be adored as the "Life-giver," the Creator. This transposition of worship from the unseen, the spiritual, to the material and visible, was easy and natural to the darkened mind and perverted heart of fallen man, and became almost universal. In all the principal schools of heathenism, from the Sabianism, in the days of Job, till now, the sun is worshiped either as really the Creator of the world, as containing a creative principle, as the residence, or, at least, the most fitting emblem of him.

The sun was the principal object worshiped as Deity by the ancient Sabians, or Zabians. Watson says, "They were probably the first corrupters of the patriarchal religion, and called 'Zabii,' or 'Zabians,' as is believed from 'tsabiim,' the 'hosts;' that is, the hosts of heaven, namely, the sun, moon, and stars, to whom they rendered worship." Dr. Townley says, "The Zabians were a sect of idolaters who flourished in the early ages of the world, considerable in their numbers, and extensive in their influence," who worshiped the hosts of heaven. Lactantius considers "Ham, the son of Noah, as the first seceder from the true religion after the Flood; and supposes Egypt, which was peopled by his descendants, to have been the country in which Zabianism, or the worship of the stars, first prevailed." "That the worship of the heavenly bodies prevailed in the East, at a very early period, is certain, from the words of Job, who thus exculpates himself from the charge of idolatry: 'If I beheld the sun when it shined, or the moon walking in brightness, and my heart hath been secretly enticed,' etc. Job xxii, 26–28." "It would appear," continues Townley, "that the idolatrous opinions of the Zabii originated with the posterity of Ham, at a very early period after the Flood, in Egypt or Chaldea, but spread so rapidly and extensively that, in a very short time, nearly the whole of the descendants of Noah were infected with their pestiferous sentiments and practices." Maimonides says, "This people had filled the whole world." They dedicated images to the sun and the other celestial orbs, and offered sacrifices to the sun. They also worshiped fire, the earthly representative of the sun. See Wat.'s Theo. Dict., Art. Zabii.

On the foregoing words of Job Dr. Clarke remarks: "In this verse Job clears himself of that idolatrous worship which was the most ancient and most consistent with reason of any species of idolatry; namely, Sabianism, the worship of the heavenly bodies—particularly the sun and moon, Jupiter and Venus; the two latter being the morning and evening stars, and the most resplendent of the heavenly bodies, the Sun and Moon excepted." (Com., vol. iii, p. 139.) "Job," observes Calmet, "points out here: 1. The worship of the sun and moon—much used in his time, and very anciently used in every part of the East; and in all probability that from which idolatry took its rise. 2. The custom of adoring the sun at its rising, and the moon at her change, a superstition which is mentioned in Ezekiel viii, 16, and in every part of profane antiquity." It may be well to add that the names both of the planets and of the days of the week, as already given, are first found either in Egypt or Chaldea, and probably originated with this sect; so that "Sun's-day," as the name of the first day of the week, is as ancient as the time of the patriarch Job.

Osiris, the first of the gods of the ancient Egyptians, worshiped as the Creator, was represented in the heavens by the sun, and in the temples by the sacred bull and figures of the sun. The *ancient* Apollo—Helius, the Sun—of the Greeks was the same divinity, though in later ages this god became endowed, in mythologic fable, with many attributes of the second person of the Holy Trinity. "There was a remarkable tradition of the Sabbath or Sun's-day at Delphi; for we are told that in the Temple of Apollo—Helius—every seventh day was a solemn festival on which the priestesses chanted pæans in honor of the serpent." (Asiatic Res.) Like Cain, these worshiped Satan in that form in which he beguiled our first parents.

The ancient Baal, Bel, Belus, or Belemus, mentioned in Scripture, of the Phœnicians, Canaanites, Babylonians, and ancient Britons, and Mithra of the Persians, was the same divinity, the sun symbolized. The Hebrews sometimes called the sun *Baal Shemesh*, that is, "Baal the sun." The name signifies governor, ruler, lord, master, and it is possible that the Latin *dies Dominica*, or Lord's day, originated in this idea. instead of in the usage of the early Christians. See Ency. Rel. Knowl. and Kitto's Cyc. on the words above.

As the sun or god of the sun, in heathenism, always represented the creative power or principle in nature, this deity, in mythology, must always correspond to the Divine Creator, the first person of the Holy Trinity, in revelation; some knowledge of whom has always existed among men. The Sabbath of Scripture is sacred to the worship of God, and commemorative of the work of creation. The Sunday of heathenism is sacred to the worship of the sun, as creative, in all these varied forms of idolatry. Both institutions do now, and always have fallen upon the same day of the week. Is not the conclusion resistless that they were originally the same? that the heathen Sunday is but a perversion of the holy Sabbath? This institution, so wonderfully preserved throughout all the religions, languages, and ages of the world, must, from the first, have been a prominent religious observance, and universally known; ordained of God at the beginning of time.

Monday, or Moon's-day, because dedicated to the moon, the second day of the week. This name is found in Saxon, Dutch, German, Danish, Swedish, Gothic, Doric, and Lapponic, Latin *dies Lunæ*. The sanctum of the "Temple of the Seven Spheres" was white to symbolize the "silvery moon," to whose special worship, under the name of Ashteroth, it seems to have been erected. The worship of this orb under different names and forms has been quite as general as that of the sun.

The second person of the Trinity was revealed to Adam as the "Seed of the woman," redeemer and preserver of mankind. As the sun, among the heathen, was emblematic of the creative power, so the moon was of the preserving power, or a passive principle in nature; and was represented in the Egyptian temples by the sacred cow, Isis, the wife and sister of Osiris, whose annual feasts occupied eight days, and is the same as Ashteroth and Astarte of the Scripture. Juno, of the Romans, was probably originally the same. A remarkable inscription is found upon Egyptian images of this deity, Isis, as follows: "*I am all that has been, that shall be, and none* [mortal] *has yet taken off my vail.*" Does not this directly refer to the "Alpha and Omega," "All and in all," Christ our Lord, not then manifest or *vailed* in the flesh, but *vailed* in mystery? What reasonable explanation has been, or can be, given of this wonderful inscription, unless it refer to the "Seed of the woman," Divinity in humanity, long before explicitly promised to the world as its Saivor, its *preserver?* That it contained some highly-important truth, widely known, is certain from the deep and lasting impression made upon the human mind. This "vail of Isis" may be traced more or less distinctly throughout Oriental customs and religion. The wearing of the *vail* in the East is more than a "fashion" or a fancy. In some way it is a religious symbol.

Tuesday, or Tuisco's-day, so called from Tuisco of the Saxons, who was their god of battles; Heindal of the Scandinavians, Mars of the Greeks and Romans, and Horus or Orus of the Egyptians; the day being named from the planet Mars, and called *dies Martis*, or Mars'-day, in Latin. This name is found in Saxon, Swedish, Dutch, Danish, and German. "The primary meaning of the root-word," says Webster, "is to press, urge, drive," as the Lord drove man from Paradise; "hence, combat, court and battle-day." The third person of the Trinity was revealed to Adam in the "flaming sword," or "infolding flame," *driving* our first parents from Eden, and "guarding the way of the tree of life;" another reason for the worship of fire in the earliest ages. As this person or presence "guarded" the literal Eden, as was known through Noah, it came to be revered as guardian, protector, and, of course, under invasion, god of war, till finally this character was generally attributed to him, and the third day of the week dedicated to the worship of him. It is not strange that each heathen nation should worship a god of battles, but it is singular that all such deities, upon careful examination and comparison, should prove to be one and the same. Such, however, is the truth. For notwithstanding all the absurdities, contradictions, and confusions of mythology seem to forbid, the chief deities of the several systems may be so identified as to form in fact but one religion; and that based upon corruptions of the true. In the estimation of fallen man, such a deity—a guardian—would naturally be regarded as cruel toward, at least, the destroyer of enemies, and thus become a source of greater corruption. The North and South of our nation, to-day, implore the same Divine aid upon each in destroying the other. If this be so among a Christian people with an open Bible, why wonder at the gross and brutalizing thoughts of the pagan? Did not the Jews falsely consider their God the implacable enemy of the Gentile world? Indeed, in the nature of things, this "guardian" would, in time, be worshiped or feared by some as the destroying power or principle of evil, as has so often been the case. It is the nature of heathenism to transfer worship from God to nature, to the brute, to the devil.

The Divine Spirit proceedeth from the Father and the Son. Heathenism again imitates the truth. In Egyptian mythology this deity, Orus, is born of Osiris and Isis, the sun and the moon. This "infolding flame" also pointed the way, through Christ, to the celestial Eden; so, in Scandinavian mythology, Tuisco—Heindal—is represented as standing at one end of the bridge that reaches from earth to heaven. There he defends the passage against the giants, taking less sleep than the birds; seeing a hundred leagues around him by night as well as day, and hearing the grass grow in the fields, and the wool upon the back of the sheep. He was also judge and pacificator, in some such sense as the Shekinah was to Israel, and as, probably, was this "flame" that "dwelt between the cherubim" east of Eden. The third story of the Temple at Babylon was colored red for Mars, the sacred color of the god of war.

The first great error, perhaps, together with Sabianism, leading to postdiluvian idolatry, seems to have been worshiping the *persons* of the Holy Trinity as individual and independent gods. In the stead of adoring all as the *one* only and true God on the first day, they dedicated the first three days of the week severally to the Father, Son, and Holy Ghost. From this plausible error to lowest paganism the way is natural and easy. In the above is the sacred *three*, the Godhead. The four names that follow, like the supposed deities they represent, have a material rather than a spiritual origin, and as their history does not bear so directly upon the question of the Sabbath, they may be treated in a more summary manner.

Wednesday, or Woden's-day. This name is very ancient. It is not the "Odin" of history, but, coming from a period more remote, is found in Saxon, Swedish, and Scandinavian. Both the name and character of this deity have some things in common with Buddha of India, and is the Mercury of the Greeks and Romans, the day in Latin being *dies Mercurii*—Mercury's-day—from the planet Mercury. Woden dwelt in the "tumbling gates" or twinkling stars. He was called the *father* of battles, not because he was the god of war, but because he adopted as children all who died in arms; that is, he received into the heavens all who fell in the service of their king. Mercury was a guide. His statutes were often placed in the road to point out the way to the traveler. Stars shine at night to show us the way. Comets also were symbolized by Mercury, the messenger of the gods. The sixth stage of the Babylonian Temple was blue, because the god to whom it was erected dwelt in the blue sky. Woden then was god of the stars.

Thursday, Thor's-day, or Thunderer's-day, Danish, German, Dutch, Latin, *dies Jovis;* Jove's, or Jupiter's-day, that is, Thunderer's-day, from the planet Jupiter. The root signifies to "drive"—like a storm; "rush"—like the wind; and "strike"—like the lightning. Thor was both Jupiter and Æolus; he was god of the air, the winds, and storms. Prayers were addressed to him for favorable winds, refreshing rains, and fruitful seasons. His color on the Temple was orange, symbol of the ripened harvest.

Friday, Frea or Frigga's-day, Saxon, German, Dutch. Frea was the Venus of the north.

The day is called *dies Veneris*, or Venus's-day, in Latin; from the planet Venus. Frea is called also Hertha, the earth, and was the giver of plenty—the queen of the earth, as the Moon was queen of heaven. Woden, Thor, and Frea were placed side by side in the order named in some of the Scandinavian temples, representing the stars, the firmament, and the earth. The fifth terrace of the Babylonian Temple was colored green for Venus, and was emblematic of the verdant earth.

Saturday, in Saxon, Seaster's-day or Seater's-day; in Latin, *dies Saturnii*, or Saturn's-day, the latter name being from the planet Saturn. Seater, of the North, was god of the sea or ocean, from "sea," the ocean, and "ster," chief, principal, director. Saturn, of the Greeks and Romans, was god of time. His son, Neptune, however, was god of the sea, and Seater and Saturn seem to have been originally the same. But Verstegan says, Seater was mistaken for Saturnus, not in regard of any Saturnical quality, but because his name sounded somewhat near it, and *his festival day fell upon the day of Saturn.* The first story of the "Temple of the Seven Spheres" was black for Saturn, representing, perhaps, the distance and darkness in which that planet revolves; or, perhaps, the hidden depths of the sea, the abode of Seater; or, the darkness of hades, where Pluto, a son of Saturn, reigned; or, yet, perhaps the oblivious post in which "Time" contains all things. It is a singular fact, that, to this day, in heraldry, the black color in blazoning the arms of sovereign princes is called "Saturn." This name also implies full, complete; and this brings these brief investigations to the "end of days," the "full" number of the week, and a "complete" summary of the universe.*

As has been said, in the first three of these

* In the above is seen a happy illustration of the sense in which the term "at the end of days" is used in Gen. iv, 3, showing that it was after Saturday, on Sunday, that Cain and Abel offered their sacrifices.

names is found the doctrine of the Holy Trinity thus preserved among men, though greatly obscured by the machinations of wicked men and Satan—also, the ancient sacred number *three;* in the others, the sacred *four*, all the realms of nature, the heavenly bodies, the aerial regions, the earth and the waters; in all added the sacred *seven*, the universe of spirit and matter, a complete number; in the three and four multiplied the sacred *twelve*, as it were infinity multiplied into itself, the strongest figure possible to represent an "innumerable company."

Could these names, institutions, and ideas have become so universally prevalent but as part of a system of religion universally received among men? Is it not clear that a weekly Sabbath formed an important feature in that religion?

FOURTH PROPOSITION.

AT THE EXODUS THE SEVENTH DAY OF THE WEEK WAS APPOINTED A PECULIAR SABBATH FOR THE JEWS.

Necessity of another Sabbath—The appointment of the seventh-day Sabbath again noticed—Giving of manna and deliverance from Egypt—The Jewish Sabbath peculiar, a "sign"—The two Sabbaths known to the Jews.

IN the providence of God it was seen fit to ordain the Mosaic economy. That economy required a ceremonial Sabbath, on which numerous laborious rites should be observed. This not harmonizing with the nature of the Sabbatic institution appointed in Eden, which was ever a type of spiritual and heavenly rest, indicated the propriety, at least, of providing another. That economy was temporary; and the circumstances requiring this ceremonial Sabbath required, also, that *it* be temporary. The demand for a Sabbath suited to this economy being imperative necessitated the providing of another than the primitive one.

The Jewish Sabbath, then, though a "rest" from ordinary labor, having many things in common with the patriarchal and Christian, was really another and a peculiar institution pertaining exclusively to the Jewish people. The original Sabbath was on the *first* day of the week. Israel left Egypt on the fifteenth day of the seventh month, in the year of the world 3899, that being Saturday, the *seventh* day of the week, which was then appointed to be a Sabbath, each year, throughout all the generations of that people, the year containing fifty-two or fifty-three weeks, as circumstances might require. (Bib. Chro., p. 109.) The fact of this appointment having been shown under the Third Proposition need not be here dwelt upon.

The seventh day is thus made the Jewish Sabbath instead of the first day of the week, not only because one peculiar to that people was required by the circumstances of the case, but, also, because on that day the Jews came out of Egypt, as Moses saith: "And remember that thou wast a servant in the land of Egypt, and that the Lord thy God brought thee out thence through a mighty hand and by a stretched out arm; *therefore* the Lord thy God commanded thee to keep the Sabbath day." Deut. v, 15. "Here," says Dr. Clarke, "is a variation in the manner of expression, *Sabbath* day for *seventh*, owing, it is supposed, to the change of the day at the exodus from Sunday to Saturday, effected upon the gathering of manna." (Com., vol. i, p. 750.) Effected, it would be better to say, the Scriptures naming it so explicitly, upon the institution of the Passover—the day of the exodus—and, doubtless, further explained at the waters of Marah. There is not only a "variation in name" seen here, but a change noticed in the nature of the institution, at least in the reasons given for its observance, as well as in the day on which it was afterward to fall, namely, the deliverance of Israel from bondage, which reason could apply only to the Jews. Observe the words, "*therefore* the Lord commanded," etc. This difference is the more striking as all the other commandments here repeated in the "second law" are the same as given on the "tables" in the twentieth chapter of Exodus.

When the manna fell it *had been commanded*, in the directions for keeping the Passover, or at the waters of Marah, that thereafter the seventh day should be the Sabbath, that "on the sixth day they should prepare that which they bring in; and it should be twice as much as they gather daily." Exodus xvi, 5. This double portion of manna was so given on Friday as to prove whether this people would keep the law, this new Sabbatic law, or no. The rulers not understanding the matter, Moses explained it more fully to them. Though the Sabbath is not here first given, the whole narrative shows that there were now some new regulations introduced respecting it which required repeated and careful explanations.

As the original Sabbath, which has been proven, was on the first day of the week, and the Jewish always on the seventh day, if any deny that this change or appointment was made at the exodus, will they, can they show when it was made? They can not. Neither can the facts in relation to this day, occurring at the exodus, herein set forth, be otherwise satisfactorily explained.

It should be remembered, further, that the Sabbath of the Israelites was a peculiar "sign" between God and his people, distinguishing them from all other nations—"It is a sign between me and you throughout your generations." It must follow that all other nations had no Sabbath, or that the Jews had a peculiar one. But it has been proven that a Sabbath was ordained at the beginning of time for all mankind, and, therefore, this must have been another. Speaking of the repetition of the law of the Sabbath at Sinai, the author of "Biblical Antiquities" remarks: "The Sabbath was made to bear something of a *peculiar* character in the Jewish economy, such as it had not before, and was not designed to retain afterward. It was invested with a certain *ceremonial* sacredness, in addition to that which it had of a purely *moral* sort. At least, it was required to be kept with a peculiar kind of outward observance that belonged only to the system of carnal ordinances which was imposed on the Israelitish Church till the time of reformation." This day was burdened with bloody rites and laborious ceremonies, and was neither a "rest" in itself, only from ordinary labor, nor a type of coming "rest."

The Jews appear to have known the *two* Sabbaths, the patriarchal and Jewish. The Evangelist Luke, in the sixth chapter and first verse of his book, speaks of a "second Sabbath after the first;" or, as the reading evidently is, "second *first* Sabbath," or, "second *prime* Sabbath." (Clarke's Com., vol. v, p. 404; comp. Com., vol. iv, p. 452, and Notes; Meth. Quar. Rev., 1850, pp. 492–4; Doddridge, Barnes, etc.) One writer calls these words "evidently a technical term;" another says, it is a phrase probably peculiar to the Jews, generally understood in the time of the Evangelist. In view of the facts now adduced, is not the sense of the text obvious? The "first" Sabbath in point of time and importance to the Jew would be his peculiar Sabbath, the seventh day of the week. The meaning, then, is, the second *Jewish* or "first;" or, simply the second Sabbath after the period given, agreeable to Matthew and Mark.

The phrases, according to Dr. Clarke, "the *Sabbath above*" and "the *Sabbath below*" are common among the Jewish writers; and they think that where the plural number is used, as in Lev. xix, 30, "Ye shall keep my Sabbaths," that the *lower* and *higher* Sabbaths are intended, and that the one is prefigured by the other.

(Com., vol. vi, p. 711.) Are not these "lower" and "higher" Sabbaths the patriarchal and the Jewish? The question is worthy of pages where only lines can now be devoted to it. The plural, Sabbaths, is not found in the New Testament, though Sabbath *days* is occasionally used, as in Matt. xii, 10–12, but plainly to indicate the weekly recurrence of one particular day. In the Old Testament the word in that form is often used.

First. For weeks—"Ye shall count," etc.; "seven Sabbaths," or weeks, "shall be complete." Lev. xxiii, 15, 16. A similar use of the word is made in computing the weeks of years to the Jubilee. Lev. xxv, 8.

Second. In connection with feasts and new moons, as in 1 Chron. xxiii, 31: "In the Sabbaths, in the new moons, and on the set feasts." Also in 2 Chron. ii, 4; viii, 13; xxxi, 3; Isa. i, 13, and a few other places. In these passages the plurality refers probably only to the recurrence of one institution, the seventh day, or of yearly feasts, as of trumpets and of tabernacles, sometimes also called Sabbath.

Third. There is another and a striking use of the plural form in a large number of commands, rebukes, and threatenings, as in Exodus xxxi, 13, "my Sabbaths," as if speaking of more than one Sabbatic institution; "my Sabbaths ye shall keep." See Lev. xix, 3, 30; xxvi, 2. "I gave them my Sabbaths to be a sign," etc. Ezek. xx, 12. When the Sabbath is spoken as a peculiar work of distinction to the Jew it is always in the plural, as if to indicate that while the Gentiles had *one* Sabbath the Jews had more than one. "My Sabbaths they greatly polluted," vs. 13, 16, 24; "Hallow my Sabbaths," v. 20. See chap. xxii, 8, 26, and other similar passages. These are the Scriptures in which the Jews say the "lower" and "higher" Sabbaths are spoken of. As the Jews could not then have kept either the Christian or heavenly Sabbath, these commands, allowing the above interpretation, must have included the proper "remembrance" of the first day of the week by offering the wave-sheaf and keeping the Pentecost, a strict weekly observance of the seventh day, together with a suitable regard to the Sabbatic year and the annual feasts, particularly a keeping of the "higher" and "lower" Sabbaths.

Will not the foregoing considerations lead the candid inquirer to this conclusion; namely, as certain as the seventh day of the week was sacred to the Jews, it was so constituted at the exodus?

FIFTH PROPOSITION.

THE JEWISH SABBATH WAS ABROGATED WITH THE JEWISH ECONOMY.

A conclusion from the Fourth Proposition—Scripture Testimony—Argument of Barnabas.

THIS Proposition is but a conclusion that must follow the affirmation of the foregoing, touching which there is left no room for doubt. If, as has been shown, the seventh-day Sabbath was an integral part of the Mosaic dispensation, it must with that dispensation have passed away.

The Proposition is also fully sustained by the following Scriptures: "One man esteemeth one day above another: another esteemeth every day." Rom. xiv, 5. (Clarke, Barnes.) "Reference is here made to the Jewish institutions, and especially to their festivals; such as the

Passover, Pentecost, Feast of Tabernacles, New Moons, Jubilee, etc. [The seventh-day Sabbath should certainly have been included in this category.] That the [first day] Sabbath is of lasting obligation may be reasonably concluded from its *institution* and from its *typical* reference." (Clarke's Com., vol. vi, p. 157.) "'One man' thinks that the new moons and Jewish festivals are holier than other days, and ought still to be observed. 'Another esteemeth every day alike'—holds that the difference of days appointed by Moses has now closed." (Benson's Com., vol. v, p. 111.) See Scott's Com. upon the same words.

The apostle Paul thus rebukes the Church of Galatia: "Ye observe days, and months, and times, and years," (Gal. iv, 10;) "Jewish Sabbaths, New Moons, Passover, Pentecost, Feast of Tabernacles, and annual solemnities. It expresses the apostle's surprise that the Galatians observed these days: 'I am afraid of you, lest I have bestowed labor upon you in vain.'" (Benson's Com., vol. v, p. 285. "Their observation of Jewish Sabbaths, etc., had the appearance of apostasy to Judaism." (Scott.)

The same apostle says also to the Colossians, "Let no man judge you in meat, or in drink, or in respect of an holy day, or of the new moon, or of the Sabbath, which are a shadow of things to come." Col. ii, 16, 17. Observe, not Sabbath *days*—the word "days" being supplied unnecessarily by the translators. Omitting that, the language is more clear and forcible, though the meaning is not changed. "Doubtless, this last [Sabbath] related principally to the weekly Sabbath, which, as observed on the seventh day, was now become a part of the abrogated Jewish law. For the Sabbath, under the Mosaic dispensation, was a *ceremonial* and a *judicial*, as well as a *moral*, requirement; the morality of it had no necessary connection with the seventh day, in preference to all others, save as that was for the time appointed; but the appropriation of a part of our time for the worship and service of God is of moral and essentially immutable obligation. The Sabbath, in the New Testament, always signifies the seventh day, the observance of which the Judaizing teachers wanted to impose upon the Gentile converts." (Scott's Com., vol. v, p. 330; also Macknight.) Attention is called to a point in an argument of Dwight against Paley; namely, the Christian Sabbath is not in the New Testament Scriptures, and was not, by the primitive Church, called the "Sabbath," but "the first day of the week," and "the Lord's day," or "rest," as in Heb. iv, 9. (See Clarke, Benson, Barnes, and compare Com. on this text.) These passages refer only to festivals and seasons sacred under the ceremonial law, which certainly have all been abolished. But there is no more reason to suppose that the law of the original and perpetual Sabbath is here annulled, than that all of the writings of Moses and the prophets are also included.

The abrogation of the Jewish Sabbath at the resurrection of Christ is plainly stated as the belief of the primitive Church, by the first of the apostolic fathers—Barnabas,* fellow-minister with Paul—whose opinion on a point like this should by no means be lightly esteemed, and whose testimony in a matter of belief in the early Church is conclusive. In his apocryphal, or rather uncanonical, "General Epistle," he says: "Bring no more vain oblations; incense is an abomination unto me; your new moons and Sabbaths, the calling of assemblies, I can not away with; it is iniquity even your solemn meetings; your new moons and appointed feasts my soul hateth. These things, therefore, *hath God abolished*, that the new law of our Lord Jesus Christ, which is without the yoke of any such necessity, might have the spiritual offering of men themselves."

* The General Epistle of Barnabas, "held in the greatest esteem by the ancients," was, undoubtedly, written by the Barnabas spoken of in the New Testament, and who, with Paul, in Acts xiv, 14, is called an apostle. (See Horne's Int., vol. i, pp. 44, 437.)

(Epis. Bar., ii, 7, 8.) Again: "He saith unto them, your new moons and your Sabbaths I can not bear them. Consider what he means by it; the Sabbaths, says he, which ye *now keep* are not acceptable unto me; but those which I have made, when, resting from all things, I shall begin the eighth day; that is, the beginning of the other world. For which cause we observe the eighth day with gladness, in which Jesus arose from the dead." (xiii, 9, 10.) How positive the statement! The Sabbaths which ye, Jews, now keep, are not acceptable; but "*those*" Sabbaths, as if referring both to the patriarchal and Christian, which I have made when "resting" from all things, in creation and redemption, namely, the eighth day, or first day of the new week, are acceptable. This father is writing to the Jews, and here applies the description given, in the first chapter of Isaiah, of the desolate and hardened condition of that people at that time to their more wretched state after they had rejected the Divine Messiah; when the whole

Temple service was "an abomination," inasmuch as that was then a perpetual denial of him. This seventh-day Sabbath being "abolished," how could the Lord accept it, or regard its ritualistic observance with pleasure?

Dr. N. West has happily expressed his views in this matter thus: "Christ was crucified and buried on the sixth day. He lay all the seventh day in the grave. The seventh-day Sabbath was buried with him, and *remains buried;* for he arose from the dead in the first day of the week when the seventh-day Sabbath was past." (Am. Brit., p. 173.)

SIXTH PROPOSITION.

WHEN JUDAISM WAS ABROGATED THE ORIGINAL SABBATH REMAINED TO THE CHRISTIAN CHURCH.

The patriarchal Sabbath reviewed—Type and Antitype—The Resurrection of Christ—Statements of Barnabas and Eusebius—Pentecost—The law of the Sabbath re-enacted by our Lord—He kept the first day after his resurrection—Argument of the apostle Paul—Example of the primitive Church conclusive.

As laid down in the Introduction of this Essay, the Sabbath is essential to the Christian religion; that is, without a suitable weekly observance of it, this religion could not long be maintained, in its purity, in the earth. The Church has not been, nor can it be, without the sacred day. Inasmuch, then, as the whole of the Jewish service was abrogated, and as there was, from the beginning, a holy Sabbath set apart for the observance of all mankind, and as it does not appear that any other was provided for the Christian Church, or that this Church needed another differing from the first, the inference is reasonable, that the Church in its wisdom, even if uninspired, would have revived the original institution, especially as Christ arose from the dead on the day of its former observance. When it is remembered that this original Sabbath had been preserved throughout all antichristian ages by very special providential care, and that in a temporary system of types and shadows requiring another Sabbath, the former, and universal one, had been constantly kept in "remembrance," apparently with reference to a revival when the temporal economy should close, the probability of such a revival is greatly increased; and when it is considered that the Divine Mind, who sanctified the first Sabbath and preserved it ever after, was the inspirer of the apostles in founding the Christian Church, and that these apostles and all the Church with them did religiously observe the first day of the week, that which in the first case was but a reasonable inference, in this assumes the nature of an axiom, it becomes certainty; namely, that this first day of the week, as appointed by God, is still preserved by him as a Sabbath of rest to all people.

It has been seen how the wave-offering commemorated the day of "rest," and prefigured the resurrection of Christ. On the morrow after the Sabbath of the Passover, as it began to dawn toward the first day of the week, while the "first-fruits" of the field were being offered in the Temple by the priest, the "first-fruits of them that slept" arose from the dead and entered into "rest," agreeable to the type. This, also, accords with the prophecy of David: "The stone which the builders rejected is become the head stone of the corner. This is the Lord's doing; it is marvelous in our eyes. This is the day which the Lord hath made; we will rejoice and be glad in it." Psa. cxviii, 22–24. Christ became the head of the corner, *after* he was rejected, *by* his resurrection, *on the day* the Lord had made a sacred festival by Sabbatizing it in the beginning; the first day of the week, on which his Church, ever after its reconsecration by the resurrection of our Lord, should rejoice and be glad. Of this passage Henry says: "It may very fitly be understood of the Christian Sabbath, which we sanctify in remembrance of Christ's resurrection, when the rejected *Stone* began to be exalted." (Comp. Com., vol. iii, p. 93.) "Of the day on which Christ arose from the dead," observes Bishop Horne, "it may, with more propriety than of any other day, be affirmed, 'This is the day which Jehovah hath made.' Then it was that the 'rejected stone' became the 'head of the corner.'" That the day of the resurrection of Christ is the one had especially in view by the inspiring mind is clear from the seventeenth verse of this Psalm: "I shall not die, but live, and declare the works of the Lord." (Horne on the Psalms, pp. 337, 338.) The Savior also applies this language directly to himself, as in the Evangelists Matthew, Mark, and Luke.

So Peter evidently understood this text when he said to the Jews—Acts iv, 10–12—"Be it known unto you all, . . . that Jesus Christ of Nazareth, whom ye crucified, whom God raised from the dead, . . . is the stone which was set at naught of you builders, which is become the head of the corner." Observe, he and his co-laborers had regarded that day as sacred on which he became the "head of the corner," from the transpiring of that event.

Barnabas, as already quoted, is explicit. He says: "We observe the eighth day in which Jesus arose from the dead with gladness," as David enjoins, and for the following reasons, *to wit:* because it is the very day—Sabbath—which the Lord had made that is "blessed," or "sanctified," by resting both from the work of creation and redemption. Speaking of the death and resurrection of Christ under the figure of the Stone that was rejected and exalted, he says: "This is the great and wonderful day which the Lord hath made." Chaps. iv, v. Likewise Ignatius, also, exhorts to the same observance of the first day, and for the same reasons, saying: "If we still continue to live according to the Jewish law, we do not confess ourselves not to have received grace. . . . Wherefore, if they who were brought up in these ancient laws come nevertheless to the newness of hope; no longer observing Sabbath, but keeping the Lord's day in which also our life is sprung up by him, and *through his death*," etc. (Epis. to Magnesians iii, 1–3.) Truly, the early Christians received the first day of the week as their Sabbath, believing it to have been of Divine appointment.

Eusebius mentions this fact on this wise, in speaking of the observance of the Passover: "There were synods and convocations of the bishops on the question"—the time of observing the Passover feast—"and all unanimously drew up an ecclesiastical decree, which they communicated to all the Churches in all places, that the mystery of our Lord's resurrection should be celebrated on no other day than the Lord's day; and that on this day alone we should observe the close of the paschal fasts. There is an epistle extant even now, of those who were assembled at the time; among whom presided Theophilus, Bishop of the Church in Cesarea, and Narcissus, Bishop of Jerusalem. There is also another epistle extant upon the same question, bearing the name of Victor. An epistle, also, of the bishops in Pontus, among whom Palmas, as the most ancient, presided; also, of the Churches of Gaul over whom Irenæus presided; . . . and epistles of many others, who, advancing one and the same doctrine, also passed the same vote; and this, their unanimous determination, was the one already mentioned." In one from the bishops of Palestine, he quotes these words; namely: "We inform you, also, that they observe the same day at Alexandria, which we also do; for letters have been sent by us to them, and from them to us, so that we celebrated the holy season with one mind and at one time." He shows conclusively that the Churches of Asia, in following the traditions of the Jews touching this matter, do plainly violate "the tradition that had been handed down to them by succession from the apostles." (Eccl. Hist., pp. 207–211.) See also Schaff's Hist. Ap. Ch., pp. 552–560; Hase's Hist. Christian Church, pp. 41, 68, 154; Mosheim's Eccl. Hist., Book I, part ii, chap. 4; and especially Gurney on the Sabbath, Appendix B, where may be found several important quotations from the Commentary of Eusebius, perfectly harmonizing with much that has preceded.

When the "day of Pentecost was fully come," the anniversary of that glorious appearing of Jehovah upon Sinai, on the first day of the week, the Spirit descended copiously upon the Church; not in a flaming sword, nor burning bush, not in clouds, not in thunders and lightnings, not in a mere type or shadow, but in reality and power, to abide like the dove upon Jesus, in "tongues as of fire," upon the apostles, to remain a quickening spirit among the people. Thus the type and the antitype are again seen in perfect harmony, making the Sabbath of the patriarchs and of the apostles as one.

Further, the great Teacher reënacted the Sabbatic law as really as he did any portion of the Decalogue. Did he say "swear not at all?" he also said, "The Sabbath was made for man;" at the same time claiming to be Lord of that day. The first is a universal prohibition; the other, according to Watson and others, a universal injunction, and an explicit recognition of the perpetual law of the Sabbath, which then and there he plainly indorsed; but he did not ordain a new institution; and as the Jewish Sabbath was so soon to pass away, he must have referred to the original one which remained after Judaism was abolished.

Besides, he seems to have paid special regard

to the first day—Sabbath—after his resurrection, appearing to his disciples no less than five different times on the day on which he arose; namely, 1. To Mary Magdalene—Mark xvi, 9; John xx, 11–18. 2. To the other women—Matt. xxviii, 9. 3. To Peter—Luke xxiv, 34; 1 Cor. xv, 5. 4. To the disciples as they were going to Emmaus—Mark xvi, 12, 13; Luke xxiv, 13–32. 5. To the apostles, in the absence of Thomas, on the same day at evening—Mark xvi, 14; Luke xxiv, 36; John xx, 19–24; 1 Cor. xv, 5. This was on the *first* Sunday after the crucifixion. Eight days after, or, on the *second* Sunday after this event, he met with the apostles when Thomas was present. John xx, 24–29.

The *seventh* Sunday after the crucifixion was made memorable in all subsequent time by the outpouring of the Divine Spirit upon the apostles. On the *sixth* probably the ascension occurred, that is, if forty entire days intervened between the resurrection and ascension of Christ, or if, as some think, the term "forty days" is used here as a "round" or "complete" number, signifying a period of six full weeks; which is indicated by the fact that the time during which the disciples "tarried at Jerusalem" seems to have been an exact week. (See Gurney on the Sabbath, pp. 76–80.) The meeting of the seven apostles at the Sea of Tiberias may have been on the *third* Sunday. The apostles having gone forth to fish "immediately" after the close of the Jewish Sabbath, "that night they caught nothing." "When the morning was come"—it may have been as it "began to dawn toward the first day of the week"—"Jesus stood on the shore." He had promised to make these disciples "fishers of men," and the miraculous draft now taken is prophetic of their future success. In the dinner provided for them, he shows that the reward of their labor is to be from him rather than in what they might gather in the Gospel net, for, by themselves, they caught nothing. On this day especially he enjoined the duty of feeding his "sheep" and his "lambs."

John says, "This is the *third* time that Jesus had showed himself to his disciples [the apostles as such] after he was risen from the dead." John xxi, 1–14. The meeting on a mountain in Galilee was, then, perhaps, on the *fourth* Sunday—Matt. xxviii, 16—and the *fifth* referred to in 1 Cor. xv, 6, wher more than five hundred brethren together saw their risen Lord. (See Barnes on the Gospels, vol. i, pp. 344–346; also, Clarke's Com., vol. v, p. 662.) Will the reader notice the Scripture account of these meetings in numerial order as just given? These are all of the personal appearances of the risen Savior to men, except to James—1 Cor. xv, 7—and in due time to Paul, and afterward to John upon the Lord's day, spoken of in the Scriptures. The first, second, and seventh of these Sundays, concerning which there is no shadow of doubt, are sufficiently marked by these occurrences at least to indicate the revival of the patriarchal Sabbath.

Judging from the life of the Savior from the

time he was twelve years old, we should expect him to meet his disciples in a special manner on the return of a weekly Sabbath while he continued upon the earth. Whether after his resurrection, which, as we have seen, annulled the law of the seventh-day Sabbath, it would be most like him to observe the dead Jewish or the living patriarchal, the reader shall judge. Since, as is generally admitted, the disciples began to meet for religious purposes upon the first day of the week *immediately* after the resurrection of Christ, and since some of these meetings were by his appointment, why not conclude that he chose for that purpose the first day in preference to all others and gave directions accordingly?

The apostle Paul recognizes the patriarchal Sabbath now revived in a manner that harmonizes beautifully with the foregoing, when he says, "there remaineth therefore a *rest*," or A KEEPING OF A SABBATH, (Marg.,) to the people of God—the Christian Church. Heb. iv, 9. No doubt, these words refer to the "rest" in heaven.

But that can not be "the keeping of *a* Sabbath," for heaven is all Sabbath—rest. Reference is here also had to the spiritual "rest" of the Christian. But that is not the keeping of a Sabbath. The apostle is, in this connection, speaking of a literal Sabbath none the less really or directly than of a spiritual or symbolic one. "For he spake in a certain place of the seventh day on this wise, And God did rest the *seventh day* from all his works." Verse 4. If the meaning of the marginal reading pertain at all to the text—that it does is clear from the language just quoted—it must imply that there "remaineth" after Judaism, to the people of God, the Christian Church, a literal Sabbath keeping, a *day* sacred to divine worship. Would not the Jews, to whom the apostle was writing, so understand his argument? So Dr. Wardlaw contends. He says, "I am of opinion, with some eminent critics, that we have in these verses—Heb. iv, 1–12—direct intimation and express authority for the change of the Sabbath from the seventh to the first day of the week. "There remaineth therefore a Sabbatism, or keeping of a Sabbath, to the people of God." He repeats, "I am perfectly satisfied as to the meaning of the passage, as an intended and explicit declaration of the change of the Sabbath." (Comp. Com., vol. v, p. 522.) This day is not, however, let it be kept in mind, now first constituted a Sabbath. No language or fact found in the New Testament would warrant such a conclusion. But that it *remained* such, after the abrogation of the ceremonial Sabbath from the patriarchal religion, is palpable.

In conclusion, the apostles and early Christians *did*, in their religious observance of the first day of the week, immediately after the resurrection of Christ, revive the patriarchal Sabbath; and as they, the apostles, were the divinely-inspired founders of the Church, this revival must be regarded not as an accident, but of Divine authority. So that the command, to "remember the Sabbath day to keep it holy," comes to us with more than Sinaitic solemnity and binding force.

To Him, through whose wisdom and goodness there "remaineth" to the Church, in all coming ages, this blessed, sacred day, as it hath been through all the past, only gathering excellence from every succeeding dispensation, be glory and dominion forever and ever!

www.ingramcontent.com/pod-product-compliance
Lightning Source LLC
LaVergne TN
LVHW011120110826
845150LV00008B/2193

* 9 7 8 1 4 2 5 5 0 7 0 7 7 *